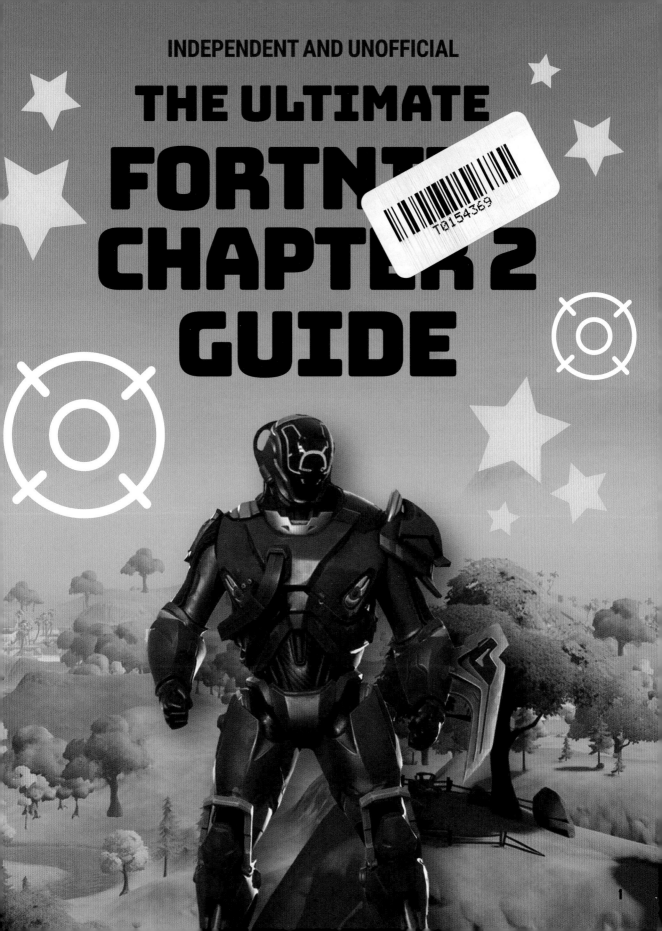

INDEPENDENT AND UNOFFICIAL

THE ULTIMATE
FORTNITE
CHAPTER 2
GUIDE

T0154369

THE ULTIMATE
FORTNITE
CHAPTER 2
GUIDE

MORTIMER

CONTENTS

The Ultimate Fortnite Chapter 2 Guide will help you battle your way through the best features of the best ever game. It's packed with all your favourite Fortnite stuff, from the weapons and vehicles featured in Chapter 2 – to skins, seasons, emotes and lots more from the game's entire history. Just like a legendary SMG, you won't want to put it down!

It doesn't matter if you're a Chapter 2 pro-player or new to the game – this book takes you on a journey around the Fortnite island that you'll **never forget**. It's time to jump in the battle bus, pick your location and join the action!

MAKE YOUR MARK!

Your Ultimate **Fortnite** Chapter 2 Guide has lots of space to put **pen** (or **pencil**) to **paper**. You'll choose the best things about **Battle Royale**, **write records**, **complete tasks** and **discover** what level of **Fortnite** fan you are!

STAY SAFE

Fortnite is an online game played on **PlayStation**, **Xbox**, **PC**, **Switch** and some **mobiles** and **tablets**. Players of different ages from around the world can compete against each other. Gamers can talk to each other, either through the text feature or using a headset and microphone, but this can be switched off. **Parents** and **guardians** should talk to their child about **being safe online** and encourage them to say if something happens that makes them unhappy. Gaming should be a fun and positive experience. More safety advice is given on pages **76–77**.

FAST FACTS AND STATS

Discover why Fortnite Battle Royale totally rules the gaming universe!

Over **250 million** gamers play Fortnite around the world. About **10 million** of these have been online and played at the same time!

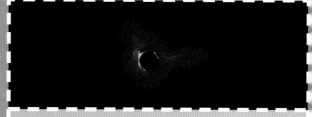

The infamous **Black Hole** sucked in the entire Fortnite game at the end of season X (season 10). The game could not be played and the Black Hole was on the screen for **37 hours** before Chapter 2 finally dropped.

The two most important numbers in Fortnite are **100** and **1**. Each games starts with **100** gamers dropping onto the island. The aim is to become No.**1**, the last surviving player at the end of the game. Good luck!

In total, there have been over **1,000** tiers to unlock in Fortnite. In each new season, buying the Battle Pass means you can unlock skins, items and rewards from new tier levels.

The shooting and survival game can be played on **PC**, **Mac**, **Xbox**, **PlayStation**, **mobile phones and tablets (both iOS and Android)**, **Nintendo Switch** and your microwave.*

Pro Fortnite players are some of the most famous gamers on the internet. Family-friendly players like iBallistic Squid, DanTDM, Ali-A and Ninja have over 50 million YouTube subscribers and gazillions of views of their **Fortnite** videos.

Fortnite has a **12 certificate** in the UK, which means it advises players to be aged 12 or older. Feel free to join a squad and have a battle if you're a 92-year-old grandma, too!

Fortnite was created by **Epic Games** and released in **2017**. After ten seasons, the **Chapter 2** version took over and a new season 1 began… but it was very different!

A new season Battle Pass usually costs **950 V-Bucks**. It can lead you to rewards worth over 25,000 V-Bucks and usually takes between 75 to 150 hours of play to totally level up.

V-Bucks

Fortnite is a massive eSport. Top players (and even you at home) can register to play in tournaments to win trophies and prizes. Epic Games dished out **$100 million** in prize money during the first season alone.

* Okay, you can't actually play Fortnite on the microwave, but maybe in the future Epic Games will release an update that will let you!

EXPERT ESSENTIALS

The vital signs that reveal a Chapter 2 pro!

SCREEN STAR

The flashiest **Fortnite** players see this tag displayed all the time. It only appears on screen when you've wiped out the opposition and secured a **Victory Royale**. If this is the first time you've seen it, you've yet to conquer the island!

FORTNITE FASHION

Outfits, called **skins**, and cool items like **backpacks** and **pets** are earned for completing missions in the **Battle Pass**. They can also be bought for **V-Bucks**. Either way, the best fighters have lots of these classy costumes and extras to choose from, dating back to way before Chapter 2 was unleashed in October 2019.

KILL COUNT

In the game screen, these symbols show the number of players you have **eliminated**. A top **Fortnite** player will be used to seeing a high number here, as their sharp shooting will be too much for other gamers to survive!

 20

 25

BUILDING BOSS

There's no escaping the fact that to dominate a battle, you'll need to be a **brilliant builder**. In the end game, **hideout structures** and **fortresses** can be the difference between victory and elimination. The complete **Fortnite** player will be able to build impressive structures in seconds!

WEAPONS MASTER

No one drops onto the island with a weapon – all **Fortnite** firearms are **looted** on location. However, an elite player will search out the best guns in a flash and know when to switch them depending on the shooting scenario. Plus they'll be adept at unleashing a lethal shot.

AWESOME UMBRELLA

If you are skydiving from the **Battle Bus** and you see someone pop open an **umbrella**, you may want to move away. The **umbrella** is awarded when you claim a **Victory Royale** as the last person left on the island. It's a **Battle Royale** badge of honour!

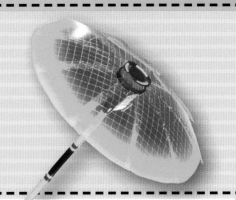

CODE CRACKIN'!

>>>>>>>>>>>>>>>>>>>>

Have you used (or do you understand) these Fortnite Chapter 2 phrases? Tick off each one that you know!

THAT GUY'S A TOTAL NO-SKIN!

Meaning: Your opposition is a noob (inexperienced player) and has no cool cosmetic skin.

THAT'S WAAAY OP!

Meaning: If an item or weapon is overpowered, then it's 'OP'!

TIME TO ADS!

Meaning: 'Aim Down Sights' is when you zoom in on a target for an accurate shot.

GG MAN, GG!

Meaning: Good game, dude!

I NEED A BIG POT!

Meaning: Shield potions, which restore 50 shield, are often talked of as a 'big pot'.

I CAN'T BELIEVE IT – I'VE BEEN KNOCKED!

Meaning: Taking a hefty hit to your health or shield during a fight.

WHAT AN OG LEGEND!

Meaning: 'OG' stands for 'original gamer', someone who's been a **Fortnite** fan since its release in 2017.

SPRAY AND PRAY!

Meaning: When you don't have total weapon control and hope that you strike the target.

WHOA, HE'S A TTV!

Meaning: 'TTV' is often part of a gamer's name and means they stream their gameplay on Twitch.

LET'S BAIT THEM, GUYS!

Meaning: Baiting refers to tricking or setting a trap for an opponent to fall for. Great move!

I'M GOING '90S

Meaning: A building phrase meaning you turn 90 degrees and build a wall each time you turn.

TOTALLY REZ ME, TEAM!

Meaning: In team games, 'rezzing' a pal means you help revive and resurrect them from a knock.

I'M SERIOUSLY LAGGING!

Meaning: My WiFi connection is causing a deadly delay on screen!

ELIM

Meaning: 'Elim' is short for elimination. When the clock's ticking, shorter words save serious time!

WHAT WAS THE
BLACK HOLE?

JUST BEFORE CHAPTER 2 TURNED THE FORTNITE WORLD UPSIDE DOWN, SOMETHING STRANGE AND MYSTERIOUS TOOK OVER EVERY PLAYER'S SCREEN...

At the close of the End Event to finish **season X** (season 10), the **Black Hole** was the only thing to be seen on screen. No other gameplay was possible, no screen options were available and there was nothing to do apart from stare at the scary **Black Hole**!

It was on screen for nearly **two days**. In total, **18** small numbers appeared around the hole at various times – 11,146, 15, 62, 87, 14, 106, 2, 150, 69, 146, 15, 36, 2, 176, 8, 160 and 65. A **Fortnite** gamer worked out that these numbers spelt out a hidden message:

"I was not alone. Others were outside the loop. This was not calculated. The moment is now inevitable."

Spooky or what?

Even though NOTHING happened when the **Black Hole** was active, it still goes down as one of the most exciting and talked about **Fortnite** events in history! Fans and players were glued to their screen to see what was going to happen.

On **YouTube**, the **Fortnite Black Hole** viewing hit an incredible high of **4.3 million** viewers watching it at the same time. On the **Twitch** gaming platform, **1.7 million** people tuned in.

When the **Black Hole** was active, players could enter a special code to play a simple space invaders-type shooting game between **Pizza Pit and Durr Burger.**

CHAPTER 2
CLOSE UP

Why did Chapter 2 send such a shockwave across the island?

>>>>>>>>>>>>>>>>>>>>

READ THE HEADLINE STORIES TO SEE WHAT EVERYONE IS TALKING ABOUT!

☐ STREAMLINED WEAPONS

When Chapter 2 arrived, heaps of **weapons** and **explosives** were **removed** and **vaulted**. Some fans liked this, others hated it!

Chapter 2 will grow and change all the time, so keep your **Battle Royale** brain switched on!

☐ NEW MAP

The all-new island featured **13 new locations** and plenty of points of interest (POIs). Turn over to see more new places.

☐ WATER WAYS

Game developers **Epic** really turned the tap on in Chapter 2, as the island is covered in water! This led to **swimming**, **boats**, **fishing** and other sick water-based fun.

MEDAL MANIA

New daily achievement **medals** became part of Chapter 2 and the **Battle Pass** system. Up to **10 medals** could be added to your **punch-card** when Chapter 2 began.

HEALING POWERS

Cool new ways to **heal** and **revive were added.** These can be used in both solo and squad play. **Team tactics** are just as important.

HIDE AWAY

Chapter 2 still lets players be sneaky and shock the enemy. **Hiding spots**, tricks and tips are always a vital skill in **Fortnite**.

BOTS BEGIN

Bots (automated robotic opponents) became a big part of **Battle Royale** after **season X** closed.

ULTIMATE UPGRADE

The ability to **upgrade** and improve your arsenal by using **your resources** is a fun new feature in Chapter 2.

CHAPTER 2: NOTES TO KNOW

When Chapter 2 appeared and caused epic excitement for **Fortnite** fans, the view among players was that the game had been simplified, stripped back to basics and generally made better. It seems strange to say, but vaulting bits from **Fortnite** – **weapons**, **vehicles**, **items** – did improve gameplay as users needed to rely on their skills and the brand new **Fortnite** features around the **new-look island**.

INCREDIBLE ISLAND!

When the new island appeared in Chapter 2, Fortnite fans couldn't wait to drop in.

FORTNITEMARES

The **centre** of the map became a **small island**, replacing the previous **Loot Lake** middle ground. Its first change came in the **Fortnitemares** LTM, when scary **zombies** emerged from its purple core and it was renamed: **Isle of the Storm**!

WATER

Waterways and **rivers** zigzag across the island for the first time. These make the perfect routes to escape along using the new **boat** vehicles (turn to **page 20** for details).

SNOW

The map's previous **ice biomes** disappeared at the start of Chapter 2, but these snowy high spots appeared to the south of **Retail Row** and **Lazy Lake**.

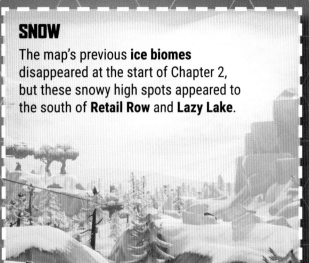

SWAMPS

Swamps have been a part of the island ever since **Moisty Mire** way back in the original **Fortnite** season 1. The new **Slurpy Swamp** zone is a must-visit area.

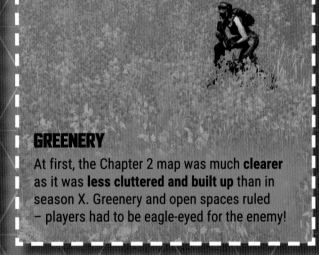

GREENERY

At first, the Chapter 2 map was much **clearer** as it was **less cluttered and built up** than in season X. Greenery and open spaces ruled – players had to be eagle-eyed for the enemy!

BIGGER ISN'T BETTER

Some gamers thought the new **Chapter 2 map** looked bigger than the old one, but in fact the area that's playable had slightly **shrunk**. That's hardly noticeable when you're out there bashing up the opposition!

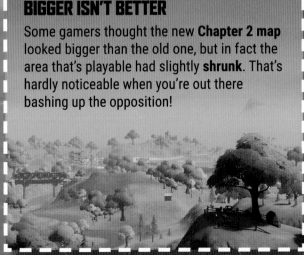

THE FIRST 13 NAMED LOCATIONS...

Pleasant Park	Craggy Cliffs
Retail Row	Holly Hedges
Salty Springs	Steamy Stacks
Frenzy Farm	
Weeping Woods	
Dirty Docks	
Lazy Lake	
Misty Meadows	
Sweaty Sands	
Slurpy Swamp	

LETHAL LOCATIONS!

The following places are just perfect for looting early on in Chapter 2 – before the storm takes hold of the land!

STEAMY STACKS

This new hotspot on the northern coastline is difficult to miss with its bulging **twin power towers** and **satellite mast**. Land here and there won't be a stack of **wood mats** to harvest, but there is plenty of **metal** and several **chest spawns**.

BEST BIT: Hit the top of those **giant stacks** and let the **rising steam** carry you along. With the lack of early-season Chapter 2 vehicles, this trick's very handy.

SLURPY SWAMP

Everyone knows the **healing** and **restorative** powers that splash around in **Slurpy Swamp**. The magic waters heal you naturally (see more on **page 71**), there are **metal mats** to harvest here and the nearby **boats** give you a quick escape. Slurpy's always busy, but don't let that put off a quick visit.

BEST BIT: Breaking open slurp kegs to boost your **shield** is helpful... and great fun, too!

< FORTNITE FACT >
Slurpy Swamp is the manufacturing centre for slurp juice.

SWEATY SANDS

Located on the north-west of the map, along a bay that contains some tiny islands, Sweaty Sands is packed with **loot chests** and materials to stock up on for a final shoot out. Head inland with the storm when you're fully loaded up.

BEST BIT: There's an upgrade station right by Sweaty Sands – these special spots let players upgrade weapons using their own resources. Clever stuff!

FRENZY FARM

Looking a lot like the original Fatal Fields, **Frenzy Farm** is a treasure trove of **hiding spots**, **barns** with **loot chests** and **open fields** to pick off opponents. **Frenzy Farm's** central location means you can stock up, then watch and wait for others moving inwards.

BEST BIT: Try using the **wooden tomato trellises** as cover when you sneak up and spy on the enemy.

PLEASANT PARK

If you're new to Chapter 2, the open spaces in **Pleasant Park** could be a **danger**. The range of **buildings**, and the **chests** hidden inside them, always attracts gamers to this **urban zone**. It also provides the chance to beef up weapons and mats quickly.

BEST BIT: The reboot van in **Pleasant Park** allows squads to boost their health.

DIRTY DOCKS

Try venturing out east to **Dirty Docks** to raid the hangers and manufacturing outbuildings for early-game goodies. It's often avoided by **experienced** players, so take advantage of its **loot rewards** before meeting tougher challenges later on.

BEST BIT: Raid the **shipping containers** and use them as a barrier if you come under rapid fire.

WATER WAY TO DO BATTLE!

Boats opened up a whole new way to travel, loot and compete in Chapter 2. Discover these brilliant boat tips and tricks.

These **new vehicles** can be found all over the **new map**, moored to jetties and buildings in rivers and coastal spots. At the start of Chapter 2, several places contained multiple boat pick-ups, including around **Slurpy Swamp**, **Sweaty Sands**, **Craggy Cliffs**, **Dirty Docks** and **Lazy Lake**.

Boats have **800HP** and are tough machines, although they'll take a steady hit each time you bash and crash them over land. Yep, that's right – boats can also be 'driven' across non-water locations if you know what you're doing! **Twin boosters** on the side of the boat is what makes this neat trick possible.

MOTORBOATS

Motorboats require one driver, but they can also carry **three** more passengers in the back, which makes them a super squad play tactic. Passengers can use weapons while being transported, so the boat can defend itself against incoming attacks.

There are two visual clues connected to a boat's **boosters**. **The loading bar**, to the right of the driver, will go **green** when they are ready to be activated. The **boosters** also rise slightly from the water and turn **purple** when they are **primed**. **Boosters** give a speed burst in the water, but also have a cool down time to stop them from being continually over used.

Boats don't just speed from A to B along the waves – they have special **built-in rockets**, too, that make a helpful weapon. Causing **35 damage** to players and structures, each rocket is fired by the driver from the front of the boat. Wait for the **three second cool down** between each round, and listen for the loading click sound to let you know when you can fire again.

SOMETHING FISHY
IS GOING ON...

Fortnite may have been a bit simpler at the start of Chapter 2, but it raised the fun factor with the introduction of fishing!

HERE'S HOW TO GET HOOKED WITH THIS HELPFUL FEATURE...

You may think that **fishing** is for old guys wearing green waders and funny hats – not in Chapter 2, though! **Fishing** serves a **vital purpose** as it gives gamers the chance to scoop up **health boosts** and even **cool weapons**.

You need a **fishing rod** to start with (obviously!). These are located near **lakes**, **docks** and **rivers** in **barrels** or can be found in **loot chests** or random ground locations. Pop the rods in your inventory, then simply cast off into the water. Be careful not to get ambushed by the enemy while your eyes are fixed on the water!

A short while after casting into the water, you should get a bite. Listen for the splashing sound and the sight of your line moving up and down. Early season Chapter 2 fish included...

SMALL FRY

A small blue fish that **boosts health** by **25** when consumed. Six **small fry** can be carried in an inventory slot and they only take one second to work on you. Small and slippery, but they can play a big part of keeping you in the game!

FLOPPER

Much fatter than **small fry**, a **flopper** carries double the power and will **increase health** by **50** after consumption. Only four **floppers** will fit in your inventory, though, so use these scaly specials very wisely if you catch one!

SLURPFISH

These awesome aquatic creatures not only **boost health** but **shield** too, which makes them the coolest catch to land. They are of **epic** rarity, so you'll need extra time and patience while fishing to pull one out of the blue stuff!

SWIM IT TO WIN IT!

If you get fed up of standing by the water with your **fishing rod**, then why not dive in and have a **swim** and a splash? Chapter 2 allows players to finally use the water to travel around, **swimming** to new locations or to escape a fire-fight. Jumping from cliff tops and heights into water also means you **don't take fall damage**. Another bonus is that you don't need to change into your swimwear, either!

< FORTNITE FACT >
Weapons can also be fished from the water. This is completely random, but a very welcome way to loot firearms!

REBOOT REWARD!

Chapter 2 dropped one of the most epic ways to revive a teammate – the reboot van!

Reboot vans were loved by **Fortnite** fans when they first appeared in Chapter 2, season 1! Playing in **duos** or **squad mode**, this **health-boosting vehicle** and its clever tech actually brought eliminated Battle Royalers back to life, with the help of a teammate.

!

< FORTNITE FACT >

Players can collect more than one dropped reboot card from a downed squad member at any one time, if needed.

Here's how it works: If you're unlucky enough to be eliminated in a team-play game, you will drop a **reboot card** straight away. **Reboot cards** sit in your regular inventory alongside mats and weapons. Once dropped, your pals have a **maximum of 90 seconds** to rush over and collect the card.

With the card collected, head for a **reboot van**. They are dotted around the island and are also shown by a **blue symbol** on your **mini map**. Interact with the van to begin the reboot process. Watch out though, because the alarm will sound and a beam of light shoots into the sky – this is not a silent reviving system!

Rebooted players will appear on the van's roof, ready for another crack at the game. They won't have their previous items and only very basic resources and weaponry, so they'll need to start looting again. The van has a cool down time between **reboots** and needs **two minutes** to recharge.

Reboot vans can't be destroyed or, sadly, driven around the map. Getting used to them, and the big advantages they have, is a great way to progress in a squad scrap. Other squad members could even **build around the van** for protection while the rebooting process takes place inside.

BLINGIN' BATTLE PASS!

Chapter 2 revealed a bold new battle pass system for players to progress through in each season. Take a look at the awesome differences!

BATTLE PASS BASICS

Let's rewind to the start and act as if you're a complete basic-level gamer! **Fortnite's battle pass** is a way to let players earn **cool rewards** in the game. The more you play and achieve, the more you get back. Rewards include **skins, weapon wraps, loading screens, gliders, emotes** (dances) and more. **Battle pass** items can't just be bought in the shop – what you get is limited and high value.

STAR STRUCK

In the previous **Fortnite** – before the bombshell of Chapter 2 exploded in 2019 – battle stars had to be collected to work up through **battle pass** tiers. You would also pick up experience (**XP**) in another season level system. Chapter 2 ditched the star system to focus only on earning **XP**. Simple but effective.

EXTRA XP

In your quest to race through a season's **battle pass missions**, remembering that it lasts for a maximum of **60 days**, there are ways to speedily gather **XP**. Easy things like **looting**, **harvesting** and finding **chests**, can give you XP. Weekly **challenges** and **medals** are the other two vital ways to scoop up extra XP. Epic came under pressure at the start of Chapter 2 to boost the weekly challenge XP from 14,000 to over 50,000, to give players a better chance of reaching the top tiers!

MEGA MEDALS

In Chapter 2, you are rewarded with **medals** for achievements and missions. These appear in your **medal punchcard** display. This punchcard **resets** every 24 hours and lets you collect **ten medals** in this time, including things like **battle medals**, **scavenger medals** and **survivor medals**. Either **8,000** or **16,000** XP was on offer for the **medals** early on in Chapter 2.

MEDAL PUNCHCARD

+8k +8k +8k +8k +16k

DOUBLE TROUBLE

One of the best things about the new **battle pass** is that most of the **skins** on offer come with another option – a bit like having an **evil twin**! So the **8-Ball Skin** could easily be switched to **8-Ball Scratch skin** and **Journey skin** could be swapped out to **Journey skin Hazard style**!

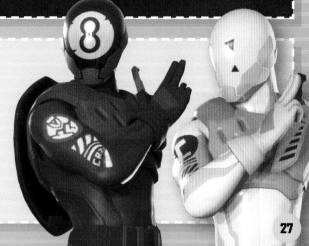

7 SURVIVAL STRATEGIES

Check out the top tips and tactics to becoming a Battle Royale boss in Chapter 2!

1
BRILL BUILDING

You'll never bag a **victory royale** if you can't build! **Harvesting** materials (mats) is the key, then knowing when and how to knock up **speedy defences**, **shields**, **towers** and **ramps**.

< FORTNITE FACT >
One of the easiest ways to quickly collect mats is to take the dropped ones from a player who has just been eliminated.

2
LANDING LESSON

Know exactly what each location offers – the **terrain**, **buildings** and **looting** spots should be very familiar to you. Don't chill out in new places for a long time until you've totally scoped out the dangers that may lurk there.

3
EXPERT INVENTORY

Always have a range of weapons in your inventory and be ready to swap in and out. **Long-range rifles** should be mixed with **shotguns** and **machine guns**, which are the kings of **close-up** and **mid-range** scraps.

4
HIGH THERE

If you're out on the **open ground**, chances are you can be picked off easily by the opposition. Head for **high spots**, like **hills** and **rooftops**, to get a good sight of enemies, but remain out of their line of vision.

5
STORM SURFING

Staying on the edge of the **storm** or just inside it, may not seem cool to some. However, this way you can move in with it and creep up on players. You've got your back well covered, too.

6
TOP TIMING

Know exactly when to **fire**, **hide**, **run**, **loot** and **build**. This comes with experience and game time, but shooting a weapon when you don't need to lets others know you're on the scene!

7
KEEP COMMUNICATING

When playing in **duos** and **squads** (unless your teammates can read your mind) you must always keep **communication** lines open. Give each other hints on what to do and where to go.

WHAT'S YOUR FORTNITE FIGHTING STYLE?

Follow the flow chart to discover which type of Fortnite fighter you are!

GET MEDS AND HEALTH

HEAD TO QUIET SPOT

START
Gliding from the battle bus, do you head for a quiet spot or an exciting new zone?

After looting a chest, do you first check your team's location or just get vital meds and health into you?

SLOWLY AND SILENTLY

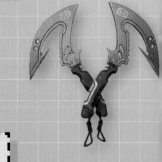

EXCITING NEW ZONE

You must move through a large field. Do you move slowly and silently or blast across on a vehicle or machine?

USE A SPEEDY VEHIC

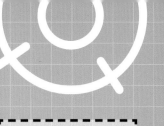

Is dropping a weapon a great team-boosting tactic or a way to lure enemies and spring a surprise?

LURE THE ENEMY →

YOU'RE A
SILENT ASSASSIN!
Moving in **silence**, using **suppressed weapons** and springing surprises on the island, is your game plan! You're a Chapter 2 fighter who prefers to work **alone** and go about your business in a **silently ruthless** way. Watch out!

TEAM-BOOSTING TACTIC →

A GUN FOR DAMAGE

CHECK TEAM LOCATION →

The storm shrinks for the final time, so do you reach for a suppressed silenced weapon or a gun that does most damage?

SUPPRESSED SILENCED WEAPON →

YOU'RE A
SQUAD STAR!
Being a **team player** and going for glory with the group is always your priority. **Duo** and **squad** mode is what you like best and if you can share **meds**, **weapons** and **knowledge** with the team then you'll reach your targets together!

NOT BOTHERED

There's a cool new-season skin! Have you got to get it or are you not bothered?

GOT TO GET IT →

YOU'RE A
GADGET GAMER!
New places, weapons, vehicles and **skins** get you motivated and up for a fight! You're a total **gadget geek** and if there's a flash new piece of **tech** or **tool** then you want to get your hands on it sharpish!

SICK SEASONS!

What makes each new one special?

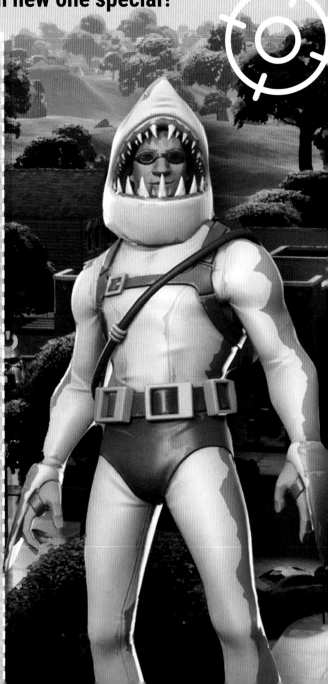

HERE'S HOW TO GET HOOKED WITH THIS HELPFUL FEATURE...

BRING ON THE BATTLE!

With each new season comes a brilliant new **battle pass**! That's **100 levels** to achieve, and over **100 rewards**, such as **emotes** and **skins**, to stash in your **locker**. Working through the **battle pass** is a sign that you're a top-level player – and that you can't wait for a new event to begin!

FORTNITE FIXES!

Gameplay mechanics are always improved with a new season – often things you never know about. For example, Epic can make the **audio** and **animation better**, **fix bugs**, **boost the UI** (user interface) and **improve streaming performance**. These may seem nerdy, but they make your **Fortnite** experience even cooler!

VAULT VIEW!

New seasons can be tense, because you just don't know if your favourite item, weapon or vehicle will be **vaulted**. This means it's **removed** from the **main game** and may only be available in **Playground** or **Creative**. On the flipside, a previously vaulted weapon that you loved may suddenly reappear.

TEASER TIME!

Game makers Epic often teases things about a new season, releasing cool **mini-clips** on **YouTube**, its website or through **social media**. Even just one little image from Epic, hinting that the next season will bring something different, can put **Fortnite** fans into meltdown and break the internet.

COUNTDOWN CLOCK!

Although there's no official set time for each season to last, they are generally around **ten weeks** each. So, for about **70 days** many players are counting down until another new campaign and map POI (points of interest) are revealed. Just make sure you fully enjoy the current season before looking ahead.

NEW-SEASON STRATEGY

When a big new update like Chapter 2 enters the game, you need to be ready to roll with the rules, modes and mayhem. These new-season tips may just help!

Don't rush into a new season, as you might put yourself in **deadly danger**! When you land from the **Battle Bus**, just **play it safe** and take a leisurely look over the surroundings. Get comfortable with any **new settings**, **systems** and **scenes**. A few days later you can head straight to the main areas and start to see some action!

Remember that any new **POIs (Points of Interest)** are likely to be packed with pros straight away. Your chances of lasting more than five minutes could be small! It's tempting to travel to exciting new spots on day one, but try to hold off and let the less clever gamers take the early hits.

Faced with a new **Fortnite** map and quests, it's a good idea to team up in **duos** or **squads**. This way, you have teammates to chat and communicate with all the time, helping you to get to grips with any new game twists. Talk about tips and tactics with your teammates!

The launch of a new season is BIG news, but throughout each season there are smaller **in-game updates**. These often go unnoticed, but pay attention to them as they can give you an edge. Updates can include things like **nerfs to new weapons** and **vehicles**, **changes in supply drops** and **glitches** being removed.

New seasons bring bags of new things, but old items and zones can also make a welcome return. In season X, **Starry Suburbs** appeared and was said to be what **Castle Ruins** was like before it was abandoned. That's a mega merging of new and old!

Get some screen time in and check out what the best **Fortnite** pros are doing in each new season. Watching family-friendly **YouTubers** and **Twitch** streams can give you hints and help on how to navigate a new zone and use new equipment to the max.

LTM LOWDOWN

Limited Time Modes (LTMs) are one of the best battles you can have! Jump in on the all the lethal LTM facts and stats, from before and after Chapter 2's release!

LTM LIKES...

CRAZY SCENES!

The most liked **LTMs** in history have been brutally bonkers. **LTM mini games** need to be totally different to a regular Royale clash – this adds to their excitement and appeal among **Fortnite** fans. **Floor is Lava** is a great example!

TIME TICKING!

Seems obvious to spell it out, but **LTMs** are only playable for a **limited time**. Usually lasting a week or so, you've got to get in there quickly and get used to the fun new game before it disappears!

RELAXED RULES!

Everything on the island is not as it seems in **LTM** games! The rules of combat could be completely different. In **Final Flight**, for example, the team with the most players left after the countdown timer expires is the winner!

BACK AGAIN!

If you do miss out on playing a special **LTM**, keep an eye out because it may return – especially if it's a popular one. **50 vs 50** reappeared because it was so loved by gamers!

SEASON WATCH!

LTMs based around the **school summer break**, **Halloween**, **Christmas** and the **NFL Super Bowl** could reappear exactly at those times of year. It's safe to predict that **Fortnite** will unveil a frightening **LTM** just as you're preparing to go trick or treating!

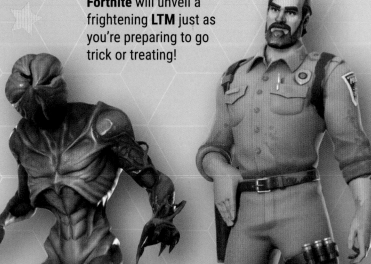

LEGENDARY LTMs...

A look through some of the most epic LTMs in history!
How many did you play?

❗ LTM: SOLID GOLD
- [ ] All weapons are of legendary status
- [ ] Extra mats gained from harvesting
- [ ] More chug jugs and slurp juice

❗ LTM: SCORE ROYALE
- [ ] Loot and collect stuff to win
- [ ] Rewards players who can scavenge
- [ ] Larger storm circles

❗ LTM: FORTNITEMARES
- [ ] Appeared in 2017, 2018 and 2019's Chapter 2
- [ ] Spooky scenes and spawning monsters
- [ ] New weapons, like the field hunter crossbow

❗ LTM: UNVAULTED
- [ ] All the vaulted weapons are in play
- [ ] Structures and vehicles return, too
- [ ] Normal rules and storm movement

❗ LTM: AIR ROYALE
- [ ] Duos compete in the X-4 stormwing
- [ ] Landing leads to elimination
- [ ] Each plane has a set number of lives

HIDEOUTS AND EXPLOSIVES

Cover up with epic disguises, then reveal yourself and cause a chaotic explosive scene. Just a standard day in Chapter 2, then!

HAY, WHAT'S THAT?!

When Epic removed the bush item as Chapter 2 arrived, gamers lost a great spot to hide in. To replace it, at the start of Chapter 2, the **haystack** item appeared for the first time. Great move, guys!

Hay bales first featured on the map near **Frenzy Farm**. Jump inside one to stay out of sight, then simply reappear behind the enemy and launch a **surprise strike**. Boom! They are much bigger than the bushes from the original **Fortnite**, but the disadvantage is that you can't move while hiding inside a **bale**, unlike the **bush**.

TOUGH TASK

In one of the early-season Chapter 2 challenges, players have to hide in **three hideouts** in three different places. Another challenge is to deal out **150 damage** within just ten seconds of leaving a hideout.

JUMP IN THE DUMP

The other Chapter 2 hideout at the start of the new season is the **metal dumpster**. This item could cause a real stink in your squad as well as your gameplay. Although you can hide in one for as long as you like before making your next move, players have quickly realized they can search dumpsters for sneaky hideaway heroes. For this reason, having a close-quarters weapon at hand is a good decision in case you are discovered.

PUMP IT UP

In Chapter 2, hanging around **gas stations** and **gas pumps** could become a dangerous decision. Epic introduced a feature where if you took a few shots at a **gas pump**, it would **explode** and inflict damage on a nearby opponent. All you need is a few accurate hits at the pump to unleash carnage!

The early-season Chapter 2 **LTM** of **Dockyard Deal** listed a mission to do just this. There were about **six gas pumps** on the new island at that time, in locations around **Frenzy Farm**, **Pleasant Park**, **Salty Springs**, **Holly Hedges** and **Craggy Cliffs**.

A BARREL OF LAUGHS... NOT!

Watch out for the mini mayhem caused by little **barrels** of gas. Similar to **gas pumps**, these canisters can also be shot at and create an evil explosion after a short while – a great surprise tactic on the enemy! Be careful if you're harvesting mats with your axe, though, as you may cause the **barrel** to go off and deal damage to yourself.

CHAPTER 2
WEAPONS

Discover deadly differences in this awesome game!

As well as the new-look map, the weapon list has also had a huge update in Chapter 2 season one. Around **25** firearms that were part of **Fortnite** in **season X** were suddenly removed, leaving about **eight main gun choices** to use around the island.

The basic weapons that remain include **burst assault rifle**, **pump shotgun, tactical shotgun, bolt-action sniper rifle** and **rocket launcher**. All of these come in each of the five variations, right from common to orange legendary. **Grenade explosives** have also stayed in play, which at least gives gamers a little more choice in battle.

UPGRADE BENCH

The introduction of the awesome **upgrade bench** was a great thing that fans really took to. An **upgrade bench** lets you boost a weapon to the **rarity** above it, so common can be upgraded to uncommon, uncommon to rare and so on. To do this, just find an **upgrade bench** and interact with it to increase a weapon's power. Here's the catch – upgrading requires your mats, and up to **350** of **wood**, **stone** and **metal** is needed to make the boost. But it's much better to do this than hunt for a rare or epic weapon!

BANDAGE BAZOOKA

The new **bandage bazooka** 'weapon' in Chapter 2 allows players to fire a bandage at a teammate and heal them by 25HP. Fire the bazooka against a wall and you'll heal yourself!

CARRY ME!

If you're unlucky enough to be downed by a hit from a weapon, a new tactic in Chapter 2 could come to your rescue. If you're on the deck and knocked, a **teammate** can **carry you** away and take you to safety with a chance to use meds. Injured players are **slung over the shoulder** – a bit like a firefighter's carry – and whisked away to a sheltered spot. Anyone need a lift?

LOCKED 'N LOADED!

From shotguns to rifles, sub-machine guns and rocket launchers – Fortnite has been a weapons fest right from its launch in 2017!

SCAR-Y STUFF!

Pack the powerful **assault rifle SCAR** and you'll be in great shape to wipe out enemies – plus plenty of buildings and structures! The **SCAR** is an absolute must for all **Fortnite** fans, with a great **medium range** that can knock opponents at ease. The **SCAR** is also not bad as a **long-range** takedown tool. Its large magazine size is a big plus.

< FORTNITE FACT >

The SCAR rifle was the first Fortnite weapon made available in common, uncommon, rare, epic and legendary class.

HEAVY GOING!

Shotties are an essential weapon out on the island, dealing deadly damage in **close** to **medium range** rucks. The **heavy shotgun** quickly became a hero gun when it dropped in season three, dishing huge damage to builds and capable of stopping an enemy with a series of well-guided tripper taps. Such a shame when Epic vaulted it in 2019!

EPIC ACTION!

Loot the **bolt-action sniper rifle** and see the other gamers scatter for shelter! It's a beast at **long-range battles**, able to one-hit a target thanks to its colossal headshot power. Make each bullet count, though, because it only has a single shot and a hefty reload of three seconds.

GREAT GRENADE!

Kicking out a crazy 400 plus structure damage, the **grenade launcher** has been a key weapon. Unshielded players could also be eliminated by a **direct hit**, but it's a tricky bit of kit to launch correctly. It also has the potential to harm the user if it bounces back off raised areas.

MINI MAYHEM!

Technically classed as an **explosive weapon** and an **assault rifle** in its time, the minigun deals out some big-time damage! It has **zero** reload time and a monstrous DPS hit that leaves enemies and buildings in tatters. This **six-shooter** looks lethal and is pretty much unstoppable in midrange shootouts. It was worshipped!

ROCKIN' REMOTE!

Able to rip apart almost anything, **C4 remote explosives** were total game changers before they were vaulted and made part of the **Creative mode** game. It needs to be placed at the scene, then shot at by the person who left them behind. Set it off and almost nothing survives its superior scatter power!

THE HEAT IS ON!

Although it dipped in and out of the vault before Chapter 2, the **thermal scoped assault rifle** remains one of the hottest bits of kit! With a DPS of 60+ in both epic and legendary, this **rocket** of a rifle has a **2x scope** and can detect enemy heat traces. It is perfect for locating hidden opponents with awesome accuracy when locked and loaded on its target!

TOP TACTICS!

The **tactical sub-machine gun** – aka the **tactical SMG** – deserves total respect. If you don't watch out for it, your time on the island won't last long! In **close** and **midrange** firing battles it's a more-than-handy hip weapon and has great accuracy for such a powerful tool. Magazine size and reload time is a drag, but one blast on this and the lights are out!

LETHAL LAUNCHER!

Also known as the **RPG**, the **rocket launcher** looks scary, is scary and probably smells and tastes scary too! As part of **Battle Royale** since way back in season 1, gamers have had lots of time to master it. The very best can whip off a rapid rocket to secure the vital **Victory Royale**. If the snarling head of an **RPG** heads towards you, it's game over!

HIT THE LETHAL LIMIT!

Some weapons have only had a short lifespan in the full Fortnite game and have mainly been used in Limited Time Modes (LTMs).

Check out the best of the bunch!

CROSSBOW

LTMs: Fortnitemares, Ice Storm Event, Sneaky Silencers

Good for: Taking out targets with an accurate arrow.

Top power: There have been a few **crossbow** versions, including the **classic** and **field hunter**, but they all strike a silent shot while causing surprise and fear around the island!

COMPACT SMG

LTMs: 14 Days of Summer

Good for: Dealing damage – its DPS is over 200!

Top power: A stunning weapon in **close quarters** combat, the **compact SMG** is a firm fave with newbies and seasoned **Battle Royale** pros. It looks the business, too!

QUAD LAUNCHER

LTMs: High Explosives, 14 Days of Summer

Good for: The end game and taking a victory royale.

Top power: Taking down towers and buildings. The shoulder-firing **quad launcher** can shoot one to four high-powered **rockets** and obliterate whatever's in its path!

!

< FORTNITE FACT >
In 2019 Fortnite teamed up with Marvel to make mythic LTM weapons such as Iron Man's repulsors and Thor's stormbreaker axe!

MOUNTED TURRET

LTMs: Playground, Creative

Good for: Scaring island enemies to death... literally!

Top power: Causing carnage to structures, vehicles and the centre of the Earth (probably!). Watch out, though, as enemies can also control the **turret** if it's left unguarded.

CREATE YOUR OWN ARMOURY

You've scanned through the best weapons.
Now it's time to create and build your own
powerful piece of kit. Just follow the instructions!

>>>>>>>>>>>>>>>>>>>>>>>>>>>>>>>>>>>>>>>

MY FAVE TYPE OF WEAPON:

Rifle ☐
Shotgun ☐
Machine gun ☐
Crossbow ☐
Pistol ☐
Grenade launcher ☐
Missile launcher ☐
General explosive ☐

>>>>>>>>>>>>>>>>>>>>>>>>>>>>>>>>>>>>>>>

MY WEAPON IS FOR:

Close range ☐
Medium range ☐
Long range ☐
Top 10 battles ☐
Squad shootouts ☐

MY WEAPON'S STRENGTHS:

Accuracy ☐
Damage ☐
Quick reloading ☐
Easy to loot ☐
Shooting on the run ☐

MY WEAPON IS AVAILABLE IN:

Common ☐
Uncommon ☐
Rare ☐
Epic ☐
Legendary ☐
Mythic ☐

MY DREAM DESIGN IS:

Draw your design here – add in as much detail as possible!

SCRIBBLE THE STATS:

Weapon name: _____

DPS: _____

Damage: _____

Magazine size: _____

Reload time: _____

Structure damage: _____

BOTS
DOS AND DON'TS

Bots are auto-controlled robotic Fortnite players that first appeared in Chapter 2. Find out some brilliant tips and tricks to deal with these human-like hunters!

DO...
Take bots seriously

If you think an opponent is a **bot**, don't simply expect an easy kill. **Bots** are not dummies and will have a similar fighting ability to you.

DON'T...
Think about viewing bots

If a **bot** defeats you, you don't then have the option of following its progress through the game. Instead you will view another human player that's part of the match.

DON'T...
TRY TO TEAM UP WITH A BOT

Bots can't be paired in duos or become part of a four-player squad game. Only real human players can do this and (at the start of Chapter 2) Epic had no plans to allow bots to join.

DO...
Make the most of vehicles

Bot players can't use **vehicles**, such as a **boat**, like you can. These drone-like fighters didn't have the ability to drive in the early Chapter 2 seasons.

DON'T...
Wait to see a bot do 90s

In early-season Chapter 2, **bots** were not able to build at 90s (placing walls at each 90-degree turn). **Bots** are basic-level builders!

DON'T...
Worry about being able to spot a bot

It makes no difference if a player is a robotic machine or not! They still class as a kill and are an opponent to get the better of around the island.

DON'T...
Fall for any tricks

A **real-life** player may try to pretend to be a bot by not building or moving well, then suddenly spring into life to eliminate you. Trust no-one in battle!

DO...
Expect bots to disappear if you improve

The basic idea is that as a player's skill improves in the game, they will face **fewer bot** opponents and be matched more with **higher-level human** gamers.

< FORTNITE FACT >

Bots work in line with Fortnite's **skill based matchmaking system** (SBMM). It pairs similar players (human and non-human) together in games so that they play on the same skill-based level.

DEADLY DANCES!

Pull out a magical Fortnite move after every elimination. These emotes are some of the best ever, even in a time before Chapter 2!

REGAL WAVE

DISC SPINNER

EACH EMOTE NEEDS...

Style!

Emotes mustn't look like a dad dancing at a birthday party – cringe! This style of dance should be sharp with plenty of swings, hip and hand movement. Dances must happen on the same spot.

>>

Swagger!

Swagger shows that the dance is confident and is something your friends will want to copy too. Careful, though, as too much swagger will spoil the show!

>>

Simplicity!

Working up an Olympics-style gymnastics routine with backflips and twists isn't going to work in **Battle Royale**! Keep the moves simple, unique and effective.

>>

Speciality!

It's important to get a memorable move into each **emote**. Make a dance distinctive from others and it could be a smash hit in the game.

ELECTRO SHUFFLE

What is it? A bouncy mix of feet flicks and crosses, with some high hand movement. Finish off with a stylish spin to perfect this shuffle.

SWIPE IT

What is it? With a gentle sway in the knees, rotate your hands around each other, low to the right and left. It's the most stylish swipe you've ever seen!

DAYDREAM

What is it? If you're a fan of the infamous Floss, then this move might be the one for you.

HOT STUFF

What is it? If you are feeling particularly smug, this move is the way to let everyone around you know it.

TRA LALALA

What is it? Get a proper spring in your step with this high-skipping move! This one is pretty simple, but it's also super fun and looks awesome, too!

GROUP GROOVE!

One of the cool new things about Chapter 2 was the creation of **group emotes**. These allow your whole squad to celebrate together and strut some stylish moves! The first **group emote**, which are also called **synced emotes**, is **high five**. It's just a simple slap of the hands, but still looks classy on the island!

FASHION FEST

Having cool character costumes, called skins, has always been popular in Fortnite. Tick off your fave skin styles, then turn over for some legendary looks!

SKIN STYLE:
Sporty star

This is when a **Fortnite** fighter is properly dressed for a game, and winning is all that matters. These **athletic** outfits can range from **NFL** heroes to **soccer-skinned** stars, tough **tennis** fans, **golfing** gamers and players who are about to go **snorkel swimming**!

I love this look: ☐

SKIN STYLE:
Dark and dangerous

There's something about being dressed in **dark** or **black clothes**, with mysterious headgear that gives a gamer the feeling of fear on the battlefield. It could be a **suit**, a **soldier** outfit or just a snug-fitting black vest and cargo trousers.

I love this look: ☐

SKIN STYLE:
Robot's got it

A mechanical monster with a menacing mood looks super scary in combat! **Robots** mean business and a **skin** that's decked out in **hi-tech materials**, **flashing eyes** and **laser-guided movement** will always be heavily purchased in the item shop.

I love this look: ☐

MATCH POINT

FUSION

THE SCIENTIST

SKIN STYLE:

Street smart

A fashion sense that blends in around any urban area. Being 'street smart' means you're good to go to battle in **buildings**, **car parks**, **malls** and **business districts**. Dress casually with comfy **trainers**, **denim**, **t-shirt**, **hoody** and **cap**.

I love this look: ☐

SKIN STYLE:

Completely crazy!

Sometimes there's just no explanation for a **skin** – it's downright **bonkers**! If you're cruising the island dressed as a bright yellow banana or with a tomato for a head, you're gonna get some stares. Fair play – you dress and act as you want and don't care what other **Fortnite** folks think!

I love this look: ☐

SKIN STYLE:

Super superhero

Fortnite often links up with movies to release super-sick **superhero skins**, such as **Star-Lord** and **Black Widow**. Other outfits defo have a strong **superhero** vibe, with powerful **muscle-packed** costumes.

I love this look: ☐

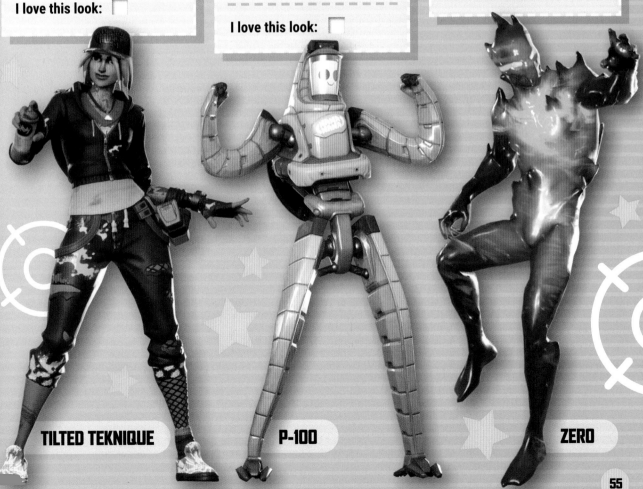

TILTED TEKNIQUE

P-100

ZERO

LEGENDARY LOOKS

Get the lowdown on some of the most epic skins ever in the history of Fortnite!

RAVEN

Possibly the scariest-looking bird of all time, **Raven's cool**, **calculated** and **lethal**. The glowing eyes come from a face that seems to have no features! The fearsome **Fusion skin**, from Chapter 2 season 1, has a similar look.

TARO

This **Japanese** inspired **ninja skin** has a white mask with two black horns and menacing bird-like eyes. The **Taro skin** belongs to the 'Storm Familiars' set and is known as the 'Protector of the wilds'. This **skin** also comes with the fearsome White Fang **back bling**.

!

< FORTNITE FACT >
At Christmas 2018, the chilling Frozen Raven skin was released, which is based on the regular look, but with full-on frostiness!

8-BALL

Chapter 2 launched with a new skin called **8-Ball** that became an instant fave! Whether you're a pro pool player or just love having a shiny head and an awesome '8' for a face, this outfit is outrageously good.

RED KNIGHT

Knights are among the coolest costumes in **Fortnite**, ranging from **Royale Knight** to **Spider Knight** and **Ultima Knight**. But the **Red Knight skin** has always stood out among the collection, with evil red eyes and a mysterious black and red colour scheme that's like nothing else. Always respect the **Red Knight**, dudes!

CHOMP SR.

With similar style to the deadly dinosaur design of **Rex**, Chomp Sr. is a **shark-suited** survivor hunting for **Fortnite** enemies. It's certainly not a fish out of water around the map – wearing this skin you'll feel like an apex predator with unstoppable powers!

REX

Check out **Rex**, the epic green **dinosaur skin**! When this first landed in the Item Shop, it quickly found itself the nickname 'Reptar'. Can you guess why? It reminded fans of the character from the classic **Rugrats** television show.

ULTIMATE ITEMS:
DOS...

Items have always been essential in Fortnite ever since its original launch. These dos and don'ts take you through all the important stuff!

DO...
KNOW THE NEW ITEMS!

When **fishing** was revealed in Chapter 2, players were soon searching for a **fishing rod** to begin pulling helpful items out of the water.

DO...
USE HEALING ITEMS WISELY

Take on a **healing** item, like a slippery **slurp fish**, when your health needs a helping hand or to top you up before a shootout. Don't waste these essential items.

DO...
VISIT THE ITEM SHOP!

It gives you the chance to put cool items in your **locker**, like **skins**, **gliders** and **harvesting tools**. Remember that none of these boost your gameplay skills, though!

DON'T...
FORGET THE BASICS!

Wood, **stone** and **metal** are three of the most basic items in **Fortnite**, but you'll need **all three** to be a **pro builder** and reach the **final ten**. Mat items also help you **upgrade** weapons at Chapter 2 **upgrade benches**.

...AND DON'TS

DON'T... ✗
GET TRAPPED!

Experienced **Fortnite** fans are often experts at laying damage **traps** in houses. Don't get lured in and end up taking a severe hit to your health from a **surprise trap** item.

DON'T... ✗
IGNORE AMMO BOXES!

The items inside one of these are crucial in combat, because you'll need plenty of **ammo** (ammunition) to power your weapons. Search for them and take what they offer.

DON'T... ✗
RUSH TO LOOT ITEMS!

When a player is wiped out, it can be tempting to rush over and **instantly loot** all their items. Just be careful that there's no-one hiding and waiting to attack you while you do it!

DON'T... ✗
IGNORE LITTLE

Whether it's a small foraged healing item, a new little item that helps you in battle or a cool trick item to fool the squad you're facing, small items all around the map can add up to make a BIG difference!

DREAM
ITEM IDENTITY

What dream item, including vaulted and original game items, would you use when faced with each of these Fortnite scenes?

SCENE: You're backed into a corner, with the enemy approaching and your ground escape options have been severely restricted. You don't have a suitable weapon to select and time is running out as HP is low.

ITEM I WOULD USE:

Jetpack ☐
Launch pad ☐
Grappler ☐
Other:

SCENE: You're having some fun in playground mode and the cool vaulted items are there to be explored and made the most of. What's the one dream item you're desperate to deploy?

ITEM I WOULD USE:

Mounted turret ☐
Remote explosives ☐
Port-a-fortress ☐
Other:

- -

SCENE: The opposition is loaded up with projectiles and explosives – they're set to cause mayhem with these items! How do you choose to defend yourself and what item is the ideal choice?

ITEM I WOULD USE:

Shield bubble ☐
Bouncer ☐
Metal (to build a fort) ☐
Other:

- -

SCENE: Your only option is to travel on foot, but you're worried that you'll be easily picked off out in the open. Deploying the right item would be a real lifesaver when faced with this tense situation!

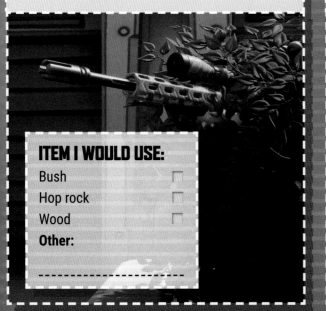

ITEM I WOULD USE:

Bush ☐
Hop rock ☐
Wood ☐
Other:

- - - - - - - - - - - - - - - - - - -

SCENE: You could really do with disappearing from the action for a while, but still be able to see what's going on. That's not easy to do in **Fortnite**, but is there a special item that can help you with this quest?

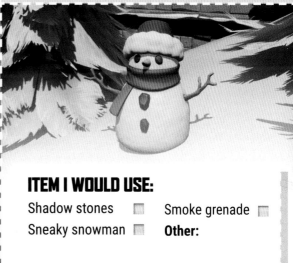

ITEM I WOULD USE:

Shadow stones ☐ Smoke grenade ☐
Sneaky snowman ☐ **Other:**

- - - - - - - - - - - - - - - -

COOL AND CRAZY COSMETICS

Time to add glitz and glamour to your game with the greatest cosmetics ever!

AWESOME ANIMALS

When **pet companions** leapt into **Fortnite** in **season 6** (remember that far back?!) they had every gamer desperate to load up with a furry friend on their back. **Pets** are just as popular now, but everyone has a liking for the original pair of **Bonesy** and **Camo**. They're cute, but don't get too close!

AXE-CELLENT CHOICE

Every gamer who drops onto the island can deploy the standard pickaxe, but it's sick to have a cool **cosmetic axe** to crunch and smash for mats! There are over **200** great-looking tools to pick from and one that always stands out is the rare **reaper axe**. Splash out **800 V-Bucks** and this scary **scythe** is all yours!

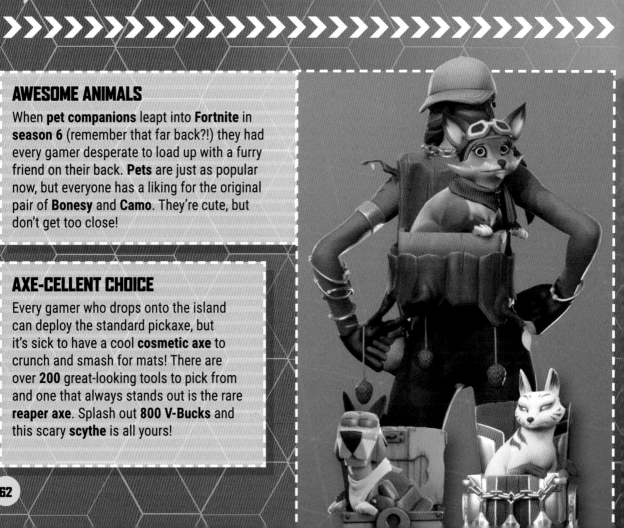

BACK IT UP

Rucksacks that you wear to school or college are pretty dull. In **Fortnite**, the **back bling** on offer from **battle passes** and the store are much more exciting than just a bag that carries your PE kit. From **wings** to **tech**, **skateboards**, **shields**, **capes** and, er, **cheese**, strap it on and get ready to bling up the island!

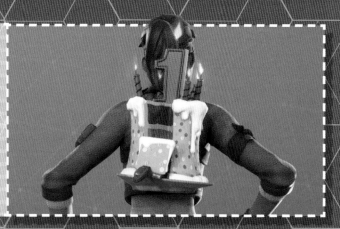

HIGH FLYIN'

Gliders are one of the rare **cosmetics** that give you a slight boost in your gameplay skills. If they're not vaulted and you can deploy it in a battle, a **glider** can whisk you away from danger. The look of a **glider** makes no difference at all, but an ultra-cool one is the sign of a high-flying pro!

LETHAL LOOK-ALIKE

The greatest **skins** are revealed on **pages 54-57**, but here's another reason why a cool **cosmetic outfit** could give you an attacking advantage. If your squad is all dressed the same, it will totally confuse the other teams and let you wreak havoc in a match. Always dress to impress, folks!

UMRELL-IEVABLE

An **umbrella** acts just like a **glider** and **floats** you to the ground in exactly the same way. However, they mean sooo much more than that! You only get an **umbrella** if you secure a **Victory Royale** in **Fortnite**. This **cosmetic** can be customized. And an **umbrella** is a flashy sign of your mega skills!

DREAM CHEST!

Wouldn't it be epic to dream up your own chest, packed with all your Fortnite faves from Chapter 2 and before? Stop dreaming and make it happen...

WHAT TO DO...

Use the space to **scribble down** all the things you'd love to discover in your **ultimate chest**. Don't just go for **weapons** and **ammo** – add extras like **vehicles**, **skins**, **emotes** and items!

MY CHEST WOULD HAVE:

< GET CREATIVE >

In **Creative mode**, players can actually load up their own **chest** with all the **weapons, explosives, items** and **vehicles** that they like. Making your own legendary **loot stash** makes you feel like a **Fortnite** god!

< CREATIVE MODE >

ON THE MOVE

In Creative Mode, Fortnite has some of the slickest, speediest (and stupidest!) vehicles ever. Take a speedy look at them.

Name: All-Terrain Kart

Top move: Speed boost when drifting

Speed: Medium/fast

Style: Motorbike-like fun on four wheels

Better known as the **ATK**, four of your crew can catch a lift in this cool machine. The passengers are free to **fire weapons** and if coloured sparks are made from the rear while **drifting**, the **ATK** would automatically quicken. The roof acts as a **bounce pad**, which is a neat attack tool!

Name: B.R.U.T.E

Top move: Firing missiles and rockets

Speed: Medium

Style: Bash, smash and crash

The **B.R.U.T.E** totally shook up the island when it appeared in season X! It was the game's first **mech suit**, with one or two players able to control it. It could fire missile and rocket attacks, jump around, stomp buildings to dust and make an overshield for protection. **B.R.U.T.E** caused huge **shockwaves** when it appeared, and not just from the damage it did every time it landed!

Name: Quadcrasher

Top move: Bashing through buildings

Speed: Medium

Style: Super-tough mini-menace

You can get your mate to hop on the back and build up boost levels that can be unleashed to smash through structures. The **quadcrasher** is fairly quick, but if you don't have enough speed to knock enemies over, it can be used to reach safe higher ground. It can even travel across water if your passenger puts down a wooden path as you move!

Name: Shopping cart

Top move: Firing from the rear

Speed: Slow (unless going downhill!)

Style: Basic, but could be fun

Carts quickly become a **transport to ditch** over other faster vehicles. They are a little crazy to control and have no brakes! As the **first form of vehicle** in the original Fortnite, they remain popular with players, especially when your teammate rides along and takes shots at surprised enemies.

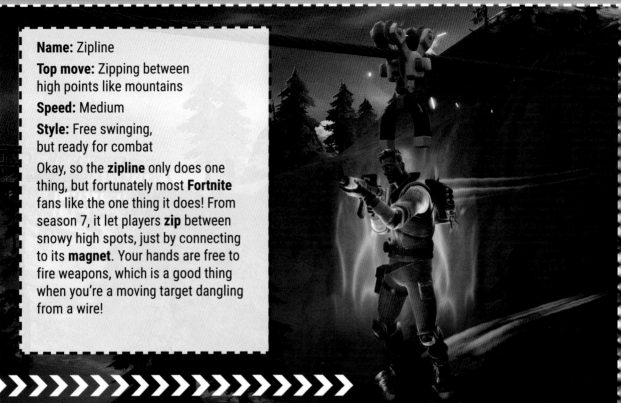

Name: Zipline

Top move: Zipping between high points like mountains

Speed: Medium

Style: Free swinging, but ready for combat

Okay, so the **zipline** only does one thing, but fortunately most **Fortnite** fans like the one thing it does! From season 7, it let players **zip** between snowy high spots, just by connecting to its **magnet**. Your hands are free to fire weapons, which is a good thing when you're a moving target dangling from a wire!

Name: X-4 Stormwing

Top move: Swooping on the enemy

Speed: Fast

Style: Daring, speedy and totally game changing

When the **X-4 Stormwing** skydived into Fortnite as ice and snow set in, it got a **very frosty reception**! However, some loved its power and the fact that five flyers (one pilot) could swoop.

Name: Driftboard

Top move: Skimming swiftly from danger

Speed: Medium/fast

Style: Nippy and very mobile

Landing at first as a transport method across snowy scenes in season seven, the **driftboard** also zoomed over **fields** and **water**, making it very practical and helpful. The user can fire a weapon while on the move, but must hop off if they need to build as the board doesn't let you construct at the same time.

Name: The Baller

Top move: Swinging to safety

Speed: Medium

Style: Secure single-seater with good protection

The Baller is a vehicle **unlike any** that have appeared on the island before. Complete with a **firing grappler** that swings the protective **ball** sphere along, the driver can escape danger areas and move into a strong spot to secure victory. Just ignore the fact that it looks like a **hamster's toy**!

CHAPTER 2
SECRETS!

Scan through these special secrets to see
how you can improve your gameplay in Chapter 2!

SECRET #1 »»»»»»»»»»

Doing a **dolphin** impression really helps you in the water! While **swimming**, press the jump button and you'll hop through the water at speed like a **dolphin**. This also makes it tougher for opponents to lock a target on you.

SECRET #2 »»»»»»»»»»

In Chapter 2, **boats** can **fly**… sort of! Use the **twin boosters** to **propel** you from the water, up a raised bank and into the air. At the start of Chapter 2, players also love zooming boats off **cliffs** and falling through the skies!

SECRET #3

Being able to **carry a teammate** away to safety is a helpful tactic. But, you can also **carry a knocked opponent** and drop them into danger! Throwing players from high spots became popular in early Chapter 2 battles!

»»»»»»»»

SECRET #4 >>>>>>>>>>

Talking of **fishing**, did you know that you can hook other players with a **fishing rod** and fling them around? Give it a go with a teammate... and against an opponent if you're feeling brave!

SECRET #5 >>>>>>>>>>

Everyone knows that wading through the **Slurpy Swamp** waters heals you, but a better method is to get into the main **Slurpy Swamp** pipe outlet and get healed quickly without being an open target.

SECRET #6 >>>>>>>>>>

Sometimes you might pull a **rusty old can** from the lakes while fishing. Don't think this is a rubbish discovery, though – cans can be thrown at enemies to inflict **20** damage!

SECRET #7 >>>>>>>>>>

The **storm** in Chapter 2 becomes easier to see through compared to the original **storm** in the **first ten seasons**. This helps to snipe and attack opponents entering the **storm's edge**!

> **! < FORTNITE FACT >**
> Drop a knocked enemy player next to a gas pump, then fire at the pump to eliminate them!

SECRET #8

In **Steamy Sacks**, search for the **power line cables** and use them just like the **zip wires** that appeared in season eight of the pre-Chapter 2 times!

NAME GAME

Just like when you select a fresh new Fortnite outfit, you can now discover what your own personal game character name is!

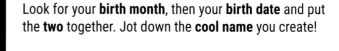

Look for your **birth month**, then your **birth date** and put the **two** together. Jot down the **cool name** you create!

I WAS BORN IN...	MY FORTNITE FIRST NAME...
< JANUARY	< WILD
< FEBRUARY	< SKYE
< MARCH	< SPECIAL
< APRIL	< TOTAL
< MAY	< SNAKE
< JUNE	< LASH
< JULY	< COMMANDER
< AUGUST	< HIGH
< SEPTEMBER	< AGENT
< OCTOBER	< SUPER
< NOVEMBER	< MAX
< DECEMBER	< MOUNT

MY BIRTH DATE IS...	MY FORTNITE SURNAME...
< 1	< PRIME
< 2	< THUNDER
< 3	< KNIGHT
< 4	< CRUISE
< 5	< RIOT
< 6	< LEADER
< 7	< FORCE
< 8	< BATTLE
< 9	< DAMAGE
< 10	< RANGER
< 11	< STORM
< 12	< BLACK
< 13	< CAT
< 14	< FLUX
< 15	< THOR
< 16	< DASH
< 17	< FENDER
< 18	< DYNAMITE
< 19	< SKIRMISH
< 20	< ROAR
< 21	< DOUBLE
< 22	< STRIKE
< 23	< BUCK
< 24	< DOC
< 25	< TEMPEST
< 26	< RAIDER
< 27	< FIRE
< 28	< PUMA
< 29	< STOCK
< 30	< CHIEF
< 31	< BARON

MY COMPLETE FORTNITE NAME IS:

----

5 WORDS THAT SUM ME UP:

\# ---------------------------------

\# ---------------------------------

\# ---------------------------------

\# ---------------------------------

\# ---------------------------------

!

< FORTNITE FACT >

There have been over 450 skins to collect and play as in Fortnite.

CHAPTER 2
RECORDS

Time to scribble down all your records, achievements, faves and facts from Fortnite Chapter 2!

THIS FORTNITE CHAPTER 2 GUIDE BELONGS TO:

....

....

MY AGE:

....

I HAVE PLAYED:

Fortnite Chapter 2

Original **Fortnite**

Save The World mode

MY FAVOURITE THING ABOUT CHAPTER 2 IS:

I HAVE:

1-10 skins

11-20 skins

20+ skins

MOST V-BUCKS I'VE HAD:

MY FAVOURITE SEASON EVER IS:

MY FAVOURITE WEAPON:

MY FAVOURITE VEHICLE:

RECORD ELIMINATIONS IN A GAME:

STUFF I WOULD BRING BACK FROM THE VAULT:

STUFF I WOULD PUT IN THE VAULT:

PLAY IT SAFE

Fortnite Chapter 2 is full of fun gameplay for individuals or teams, but it's important to stay safe online while playing. These tips and suggestions will help gamers and parents.

VOICE CHAT

In Fortnite, players can **chat** to other players if they are using **headphones** and a **microphone**. This is automatically switched on, but can be switched off, so that others can't chat with you. To do this, go to 'menu', then 'settings' and the 'audio' icon.

PARENTAL PICKS

There are lots of **parental controls** that an adult can apply to Fortnite settings, allowing the player to be able to do or not do certain things. The **parental controls** tab is accessed through the lobby area. These include language filter (for text chat), auto decline friend request and hide your name settings.

SHARE IT

Parents, guardians and **adults** around you will be interested to know what Fortnite is all about. Talk to them about the game, what it involves and how you are progressing. It'll help them understand why you like the game and set **basic rules** between you about when and how long you can play for. Setting up your **console** and **screen** in a place in the house where adults can see and hear you play is a good idea.

REPORT IT

If something happens in Fortnite that **upsets** you, or someone acts in an **inappropriate** way towards you, don't keep it to yourself. Talk to a **parent** or **guardian** about what happened – they can then offer advice about what to do and help you feel better.

BAD BEHAVIOUR

Epic has a **code of conduct**, which is like a set of player rules to make **Fortnite** fun and friendly. If you think a player has done something bad during a game, it can be reported straight away to Epic. From the menu item, select 'report player' and then the player's name, your reason and any additional info to tell Epic.

PASSWORD POWER

When setting up **passwords** and **usernames** for Fortnite Chapter 2, make sure you do this with your **parent** or **guardian**. **Passwords** need to be strong, but memorable, and usernames must not include both your first and surname. Ask your grown up to make a note of it.

PLAYTIME REPORT

Also through the **parental controls** option, a setting called a **weekly playtime report** can be switched on. This sends an email to the email address connected to the account, summarizing the **activity** of the player over the previous **seven days**.

< FORTNITE FACT >

Having the sound up, on your monitor or console will mean other people around you at home will hear what's happening and being said. This can assure them that nothing inappropriate is happening.

CHAPTER 2
QUIZ

Now that you've explored the wonders of Chapter 2, it's time to put your knowledge to the test! Let's quiz...

1 >>>>>>>>>>>>>

What pass do you need to buy to access the skins, items and rewards from new tier levels?

a) Battle Pass

b) Bucks Pass

c) Trophy Pass

>>>>>>>>>>>>>>

2

How many million gamers are playing Fortnite around the world?

a) 200 million

b) 250 million

c) 20 million

3

What age certificate does Fortnite have in the UK?

a) 12

b) 15

c) 18

4

What event happened to stop people being able to play Fortnite for 37 hours before Chapter 2?

a) The Blue Hole

b) Bots Takeover

c) The Black Hole

5

What is awarded when you claim a Victory Royale as the last person left on the island?

a) Firearms

b) Teapot

c) Umbrella

6

What does LTM stand for?

a) Limited Town Models

b) Limited Time Models

c) Limited Time Mode

7

The auto-controlled Fortnite players which first appear in Chapter 2 are called...

a) Robos

b) Bots

c) Robotics

8

Which of the below is not a Fortnite emote?

a) Dabstand

b) Tra lalala

c) Cold stuff

9

Name the first ever weapon available in common, uncommon, rare, epic and legendary class.

a) SCAR rifle

b) Minigun

c) C4 remote explosives

CHAPTER 2: QUIZ
ANSWERS

| 1a | 2b | 3a | 4c | 5c | 6c | 7b | 8c | 9a |

'CARRY' ON
THE BATTLE,
DUDES!